A Golfer's Guide to Enlightenment

W.T. Firth

Shaun,
Happy Holidays and
may you find inspiration
& wisdom in this book
written by one of my dear
friends.
Fehrunisa

Book design by: Mike Kitson
Cover Art & Design by: John Romanchuk
Back Cover Design by: Alex Leutzinger
Editing: Cindie Geddes & Professor Laird Blackwell

Destiny Press
COPYRIGHT © 2002, Destiny Press
All rights reserved
Printed in the United States of America
02 01 00 99 98 12 11 10 9 8 7 6

Library of Congress Catalog Card Number: *In Progress*
ISBN 0-9722000-0-2

Dedicated to those who play the game,
and to my beloved guru—Golf.

Email comments to:
cosmicgolfer@gbis.com

Visit our Website:
www.cosmicgolfer.com

Acknowledgments

With love and respect, I give thanks to the following:

My dad, who introduced me to the game of golf. Mom, you are my gift of unconditional love.

Eddie Duino and Gary Cursio, you opened the door and welcomed me into the realm of professional golf. Lane Lewis, I am indeed grateful for such a beautiful place to work and play. Garrett Good, P.G.A. Member and Head Golf Professional, thank you for your professionalism, counsel, and friendship .

Helene Yates, thank you for all those hours of computer time and editing of "a golfer's journey." Margie Lapanja and Mike Tremayne, I sincerely appreciate your comments and evaluation.

Blessings to my editors Cindie Geddes and Professor Laird Blackwell.

Julia Cameron, I applaud you and your inspirational book, "The Artist's Way."

Most of all I wish to thank my heart's love— Joy. You are my faith in what is divine.

Contents

Author's Note

Golf may be a game
but for me, it is a path.
I am of the golfing tribe.
Each round is a journey—
a bridge to the universal wisdom.
These writings are a journal
of my travels.

W.T. Firth

Inward

To say "I am a golfer," is to say
"I am a traveler."
You may ask, "To where do you travel?"
I would answer, "To my Self."

Beyond the personality.

Education

Each round of golf is a teaching.
To learn the lessons …
I must be available.

I am accessible when I am in my body,
feeling the earth, and receptive to guidance.

The Kiss

To have stumbled and fallen down—
It was the ground calling.
Sometimes the path is invisible
until I am facing it.

Humility is medicine for the golfer's ego.
It is also a call to the present.
*A fresh start begins **now**.*

Flow

As a golfer, I relate to the shifting elements
and act accordingly.
No matter the bounce, whatever the lie,
I say hello and go to work.

Opportunity has many disguises.

Rapids Ahead

The lie of the ball,
the lay of the land,
the confidence of attitude …
observe them well and proceed.

A knowledgeable guide will scout the hazards.

Worthy Questions

Where do I want to hit this shot?
Am I being realistic?
If I imagine myself doing it successfully,
what will it feel like?
Did I maintain focus until flight was in sight?
Was I educated by the experience?

*Clarity of intention, truth, imagination, feeling,
determination, and understanding are
the keys which unlock my true potential.*

Anywhere

If I have no destination in mind for the intended golf shot, "everywhere" becomes my target.

Once in a while this is a good practice.
I will always hit my target.

Familiar Territory

If my mind is in one place
and my body in another,
where am I?

*I allow my body to feel the golf shot
my mind is imagining. I am present.*

Hello

Am I playing the golf course,
or is the golf course playing me?

*It is okay to give a nod to the architect
and to the staff who maintain the course.*

Satisfaction

To be present, feeling the moment,
free from judgment is how the ordinary
becomes magical,
glistening in its simplicity.

Unveil, and allow the golf course to greet you.

Revelation

When I am present with silence,
I touch the stillness of peace
and hear the whispers of insight.
I am engaged with reality.
Now is the time to focus on the shot at hand.

Inspiration will guide my movements.

Favorite

One shot equals one stroke. Each one is as important
as the next. When I start playing favorites—thinking
this shot is more important than the others—my
"extra concentration" usually backfires.
I left my natural rhythm for a strained effort.
Now my other shots rebel because they don't
feel as special.

*Golfers often confuse "concentration" with "trying really
hard." One is focused on the impending intention; the other
is a focus on effort.*

Swish or Bank

Clarity of intention is of the utmost importance for a successful shot. If I'm not sure whether to lay up or go for it, my success is in doubt.

If I get caught in between, the only points I'll score will be the higher numbers on my scorecard.

Secret Code

Are my swing-thoughts
fragments of impending chaos
or passwords which serve to unify
the mind and body?

To grasp the value of my mental dialogue,
I need only observe the outcome of my shot.

Return to Go
(or go directly to jail)

When commitment is distracted and
then followed by a convincing voice
saying: "You can do it," it would be
wise to start at the beginning and recommit.

Ego's intention may be gallant,
but it is I who must hit the shot.

Ego Speaks

Water at the left:
"I feel like I'm about to pull it left."
"Just aim more right or play the ball
back in your stance. Trust it!"
Splash!

The next hole:
"Hit the driver, aim down the middle,
you'll hit this one straight."
"But I feel like I'm going to hook it."
"Just keep your right hand passive. You can do it!"
Hooked o.b.!

When I'm tricked by the convincing voice of ego,
I will use humor to clear the message.

Puppet Strings

My internal dialogue has the unique ability to capture my attention (under the disguise of advisor), sabotage the endeavor at hand, and then receive applause for its commentary on what went wrong.

Hindsight is not a golfer. It is time for the sword.

Static

"See all of those white stakes? Whatever you do, don't go left! It's a long par four, so hit your driver, but don't hook it! Here we go—be cool, stay focused. Full shoulder turn, but keep your left heel down. Rotate; remember, don't sway on the backswing, left side leads, watch your spine angle, low and slow on the take-away, one piece. Here we go—don't go left!"

"Unbelievable, I blocked the shot dead right!"

"Well, you didn't go left. You came out of your posture. You didn't fire your right knee, so on this next shot…."

Double bogey!

Conflict

It seems my subconscious has selective hearing, often missing the "don't" part of my commands.

"Don't hit this putt too hard." See ya!

Now my subconscious is perplexed by my anger, having given me what I asked for!?

Time to shift my communication tactics.

Negative

To say, "I don't want" is to immediately go there.

"Don't hit it in the water." Splash!

I have imagined where I don't want
to go, so by the time I've said "I don't"
I'm already returning from having gone there.

The question is "will I go back?"

Trust

Trying to control my golf swing
through mind talk is to lose control
both physically and mentally.
I will reaffirm my intent and allow
my body to perform.

Faith is silence in action.

Mind or Heart

When desires become demands,
they will turn into anger if not met.

A shift in attitude will change
the corresponding outcome.

*I will aspire to attain my goals, and I will learn from
all of my experiences; good or bad, they will teach me.*

Trickster

When I hear my internal dialogue
debating why I should ... or should not ...,
this is rationalization. It sends my golf shot
into the trees, rough, water, o.b.,
or some other unwanted destination.

That which knows has no need to rationalize.
                                        -Wisdom

Bubbles Will Pop

There is no need to fight unwanted thoughts.
Once they surface, they are exposed and vulnerable.
Compassion will melt them.
Now I am free to focus on the shot.

My heart is a muscle. I must use it constantly.

Flame On

A golfer's use of the affirmation is often in the negative:

"I can't buy a putt."
"I never get a break."
"I just don't have it today."
"These greens are so slow."

Words reveal attitude.
If it's anger that calls,
I will use it to breathe fire into a commitment.

Illusions

"I lost it!
This is the worst I've....
It works every time but....
I could have ... I should have....
All I have to do is keep my head down.
I know what I'm doing wrong.
That's it!"

You are not an it, and neither is truth.
Change is the dance of reality.

Blind

I watched the old man take two full distinct practice swings, followed by several waggles before hitting his shot. His wife (who was standing nearby) said, "Good shot, honey; see what happens when you don't take any practice swings!"

I wondered how often I've tricked my mind to not see. Had his shot been a bad one, would she have seen the practice swings?

Redial

Am I practicing a habit that is sending
my ball away from the target?

*The right golf instructor can evaluate
the productivity of my practice in a matter
of minutes. It could save years of frustration,
but only to the extent to which I am willing to change.*

Lizard

Optical illusion will lead me right of parallel
(I swing right-handed) if I lose focus of my target line.
Perhaps it would be easier if I had eyes on
the sides of my head.

*Once I master the alignment of parallel,
the task of swinging on the inside path is basic.*

Well-Being

Basically, the shot is over before the club begins its backswing. In other words, it's what I bring to the shot that produces the outcome.

A calm mind and my best posture are what I bring with me. Worry, doubt, and fear are not invited.

Present

I am perplexed.
Why is it so?
Yesterday's discoveries now hook or fade away.
They seemed so true and simple.
I thought for sure I knew.
But then came today.
Why do I struggle?

Is it possible
that when I think I know,
a door closes?
I am no longer open,
until I am forced to move.
Now my complacency is disturbed.

Visions of the past rain on today.
I stumble, lost in a mental maze,
until my eyes can see
that there are no clouds in the sky.

This moment welcomes me back.

A Perfect Swing

The rhythm of true flow must change—
that's what the moon says.

Yesterday a seven-iron was perfect, but today....

Harmony

Anyone can get upset;
there are plenty of bad lies.
But rare indeed are those
who allow what is, to be.

Some of my best shots came from a bad lie;
good karma came from playing the shot as it lay.

Tantrums

I must resist the temptation to whine.
The golf gods are not against me.
There are dues to be paid and no one escapes.

Character development 101.

Faith

The stronger my attachment to a
desired outcome,
the deeper the conflict
when reality sends my shot off
to some other destination.

I will resolve my conflict by accepting what is.

Productivity

Instead of caring so much about what may happen,
I will allow myself to care for what is happening.

The feelings involved when I put my hands on the
club—the way I move my body to soothe its
tensions—is how I care.

Once I determine the shot to be played,
my mind is just a silent passenger.

Tangents

It's easy to get lost in a maze of concepts.
A few errant shots and my mind
begins a quest … destination unknown.

*When I feel my feet on the ground, find my breath,
and use it to soften my belly, I am back.*

A Method

Breathe.
Observe and feel surroundings.
Formulate plan.
Listen past ego.
Choose club.
Aim club and body; set angles.
Release tensions through
breath and body movements.
Release hope and expectations.
Before any thought returns—fire!

Enjoy the ride!

Remembrance

What do my eyes see when they look at the golf ball?
Sometimes the ball. But there are times when
doubt or fear capture my vision.
This leads to a restriction of my natural body flow.
No longer am I conscious of a target destination.
I'm not even conscious that I have fallen into a void.

*The golf ball is my reminder of contentment
and destination.
The ball rests, simply being. I look into its core
and there, like a crystal ball, the image of my target
appears. At this moment, before I lose the vision,
my club begins its backswing.*

Spotlight

"And now on the first tee…."
You hear your name announced.
The gallery looks on with anticipation.
A silence deepens as your eyes scan the fairway.
You see your destination with such clarity that the
image is etched into your mind. With pure attention
you aim the clubface and move your body into a
perfectly aligned posture. You feel tall, yet centered
and grounded. Heaven and earth are aligned.
The pulse of your nervous system is congruent with
the feeling of the motion you are about to perform.
All systems are ready. Commitment releases the shot;
energy in motion takes flight.

A star is born.

Destiny

Golf is a game that presents the opportunity
to transcend the mundane, to ride the imagination,
and to feel the pulse of the divine.

*With a sense of wonder I greet this moment
and those yet to come, grateful to be alive.*

Depth

Turbulence is on the surface,
especially when the wind blows.
But I run deep, my current is strong.
I am an ocean.

Good shot; bad shot.
They are simply waves crashing on an empty beach.
I play golf because I am a golfer.

Microcosm

Blake saw the macrocosm in a grain of sand,
Whitman in a blade of grass.
As a golfer, I see both.

Visible infinity.

Birth

Each time I write or draw,
I am both part of and witness to
an act of creation; the mental realm
becomes physical.

*The golf course is my canvas, the golf swing my brush.
My intent will soon be born.*

MC^2

The formulation of a golf shot requires intelligence and passion. There is the alignment of club and body angles plus the alignment of heart and will. Add the elements of nature and a bit of luck. Subtract the critical voice. Walk on. Golf = Math + Art.

I am a golfer; I am also a relativist.

Creating a Déjà Vu

I use my mind's eye to visualize my body,
my posture, and the mannerisms I will use.
Next, I feel the shot
and stay connected to that feeling!

I pretend with conviction.

Mind's Eye

When imagination captures attention,
the outside disappears.
Now the question is: What am I imagining?
Do I see the shot flying high or low,
fading or drawing?
How fast is the ball rolling as
it falls over the edge and
drops to the bottom of the cup?

I am oblivious to whomever may be watching.
I wrote the script; the cameras are rolling—Action!

Blood Pressure

Fear in rock climbing is of the body.
One false move and I'm off to the hospital.
Fear in golf is of the mind.
A few double bogies, and it's off
to the mental ward.

*The hazards of the golf course can only
threaten the scorecard.*

Insight

The golf course is full of illusions.
The golfer must be willing to see past logic;
common sense is not enough.

Intuition: the inspiration that leads me to truth.

Mirage

Illusion or fact does not matter
if the body believes what the
mind is perceiving.

*A coiled piece of rope may look like a snake
ready to strike; white stakes (o.b.) may appear
to have teeth. I must remember wood doesn't bite!*

Storm Brewing

Do white stakes represent danger?
Does sand or water cause a tremble?
Obstacles will always be present
in the endeavor.
I acknowledge their presence and
steer my course.

There are times when I must simply "ship the oars".

Easy

The lay-up shot is not hampered by
the dominance of performance pressure.
This freedom mobilizes the body,
often adding ten yards of extra distance.

*Today I shall consider most
of my golf shots as lay-ups.*

Grip Pressure

One day while watering the lawn,
I realized that the stream of water
went farther and more directly to where
I aimed it when I didn't squeeze
the handle to its maximum.

Less can be more.

Witnessing My Best Shot

When I go to that place,
finally I give up all hope,
and for a moment there is no trying.

This is where my true flow is allowed to exist.

Doing vs. Trying

A really good shot just seems
to happen effortlessly.
A really bad shot requires extra effort!

*Quick and tight with all my might
equals the distance of an elephant's flight.*

Discovery

A golf lesson is any experience which serves to awaken my mind from illusion.

A similar situation will soon appear to check on my understanding. Beware of complacency.

The Set-Up

When I think I've discovered a secret
about my golf swing,
this is a signal that it may soon be departing,
especially if I tell anyone.

Seeds of insight illume,
but require time to mature.

Duality

It seems that whenever a golfer proclaims a certainty, the birth of its opposite takes place.

Close the screen, but keep the door open.

Acceptance Speech

… five stroke lead with three to play …

"I'd like to thank…."
"Now I can buy that…."
"Just don't choke, it's in the bag unless…."
"Move over boys, your new champion
is coming home."

Triple / Double / Bogey / Tied for second.

Competition

Playing in golf tournaments is the best way to see how solid your golf swing is. Pressure will call everything out of the closet to confront any weakness of mind and body.

Everyone feels the throat tighten, except those who don't show up or are not in contention.

Onward to the Present

A low score could be detrimental to
my future enjoyment of the game,
but only when I compare or expect
the future to be the same as the past.

*The party must eventually end,
and this too will be temporary.*

Score Keeper

A number is simply a number.
That is until it's written on my scorecard.
Now, how much power do I give that number?

The more attention I pay to my score, the faster it grows.
I am present with this shot....

Not Decaf

When I'm unfocused, it's as though a fog has
infiltrated my mind.
This state affects my body, producing a listless feeling
and a golf shot that lacks intent.

*A remedy for the comatose moment is to wear
a rubber band on my wrist. To wake up,
I stretch it out and let it snap. Yeeow!*

Sweet Spot

There is a certain resonance when the club
contacts the ball. The deeper tones send
a vibration that feels good in my body.
I'll practice hitting different spots on the clubface
(toe, heel, low, middle, and high) to help me
recognize the vibe and feel of the sweet spot.

I will imagine the sound I would like to play.

Forever

Imagine having a goal of learning to play
the violin. You take one 45-minute lesson
once a week, but do not practice in between.
How long do you think it will take you
to become an accomplished violinist?

*The game of golf is comparable in its complexities;
this is why I must practice.*

Posture

Take a moment and attend to how you
are sitting at this very moment. Is your
spine long and upright?
How about your neck and head position?
Are your feet flat on the ground?
There are no wrong answers, just the facts.

*The way you occupy your body affects the outcome of your
golf shot (not to mention your health and well-being).
Observe how you walk and then see if you can add some
cat-like grace to your movements.
Stand as though the ground were rising up to support you.
Allow your weight to be distributed in accordance with the
shot at hand.
Without your body, how far could you hit the ball?*

Sensation

Breathe in and out through your nose.
Is the air being divided equally
between your nostrils?
Can you intentionally direct the
flow (more or less to either side) with your will?

*When you can answer "yes" to these questions,
and then apply this awareness, sensitivity, and intention
to your golf game … I will call you "Captain."*

The Other Brain

Within my body there is a center.
It rests approximately two finger-widths
below my navel. I go inside,
and from that place my swing begins.
This is how I tap into my strength
and remain centered.

Breathe the belly.

Unity

Rhythm and balance will happen
when the mind and body
hear the same music.

When I feel an internal rhythm,
a sense of pulse or beat,
my golf swing will not be constricted
by a chattering mind.

Zorba

My body is flowing liquid. If the flow is restricted,
stagnation begins, followed by calcification.
To counter this process I must play golf:
release attitudes and opinions
that are becoming fossilized,
reclaim my sense of humor, and
give and receive frequent massages.

Life is a dance.

Multiple Choice

The golf course may be:
a. a playground,
b. a battlefield,
c. a circus,
d. a therapy session,
e. all of the above.

Each game offers a multitude of experiences.
There is no wrong answer.

Enlightenment

It has been said, "If you want to know someone,
simply play a game of golf with them."

I asked the golfer, "are you enlightened?"
"No … yes …
No, I am not enlightened when I think I am.
Yes, I am enlightened—when I don't think … I am."

T. Firth
2002